GW01374596

Welcome to Slovenia, a magical country in the heart of Europe. It has sparkling lakes, tall green mountains, fairytale castles, and friendly towns. People here speak Slovene and love their music, food, and nature. Even though Slovenia is small, it has a big story filled with ancient history, brave people, and amazing places. Over time, it has been home to cave dwellers, Roman cities, and kings in castles. Get ready for an adventure through forests, rivers, and stories. Let's explore Slovenia from the past to the present!

Thousands of years ago, the first people lived in what is now Slovenia. They made their homes in caves, hunted animals, and used stone tools. Archaeologists found some of the oldest bones and tools in places like Potok Cave. One special find was a flute made from a bear's bone, believed to be over 40,000 years old. That makes it the oldest musical instrument ever discovered. These early people didn't have cities or castles, but they started the story of Slovenia. They followed the rivers, listened to the wind in the trees, and sang songs by the fire.

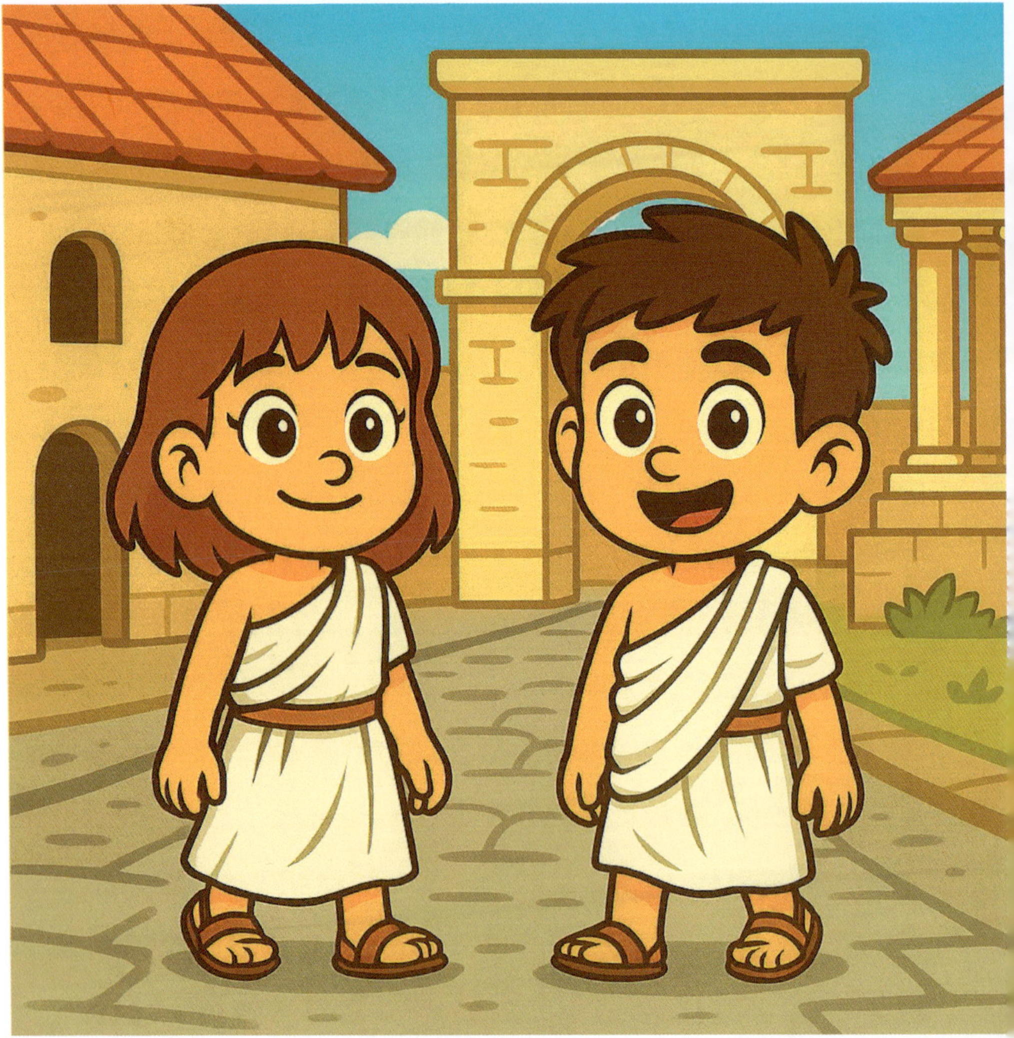

Long ago, the Romans built a city called Emona where Slovenia's capital is today. Emona had strong stone walls, grand buildings, and busy markets. Roman people wore togas, spoke Latin, and took baths in warm bathhouses. They brought roads, laws, and trade to the area. You can still see Roman ruins in Ljubljana, like ancient walls and stones with carvings. The Romans helped shape the land for hundreds of years. It was a time of soldiers, emperors, and ideas that traveled from Rome to the edge of the Alps.

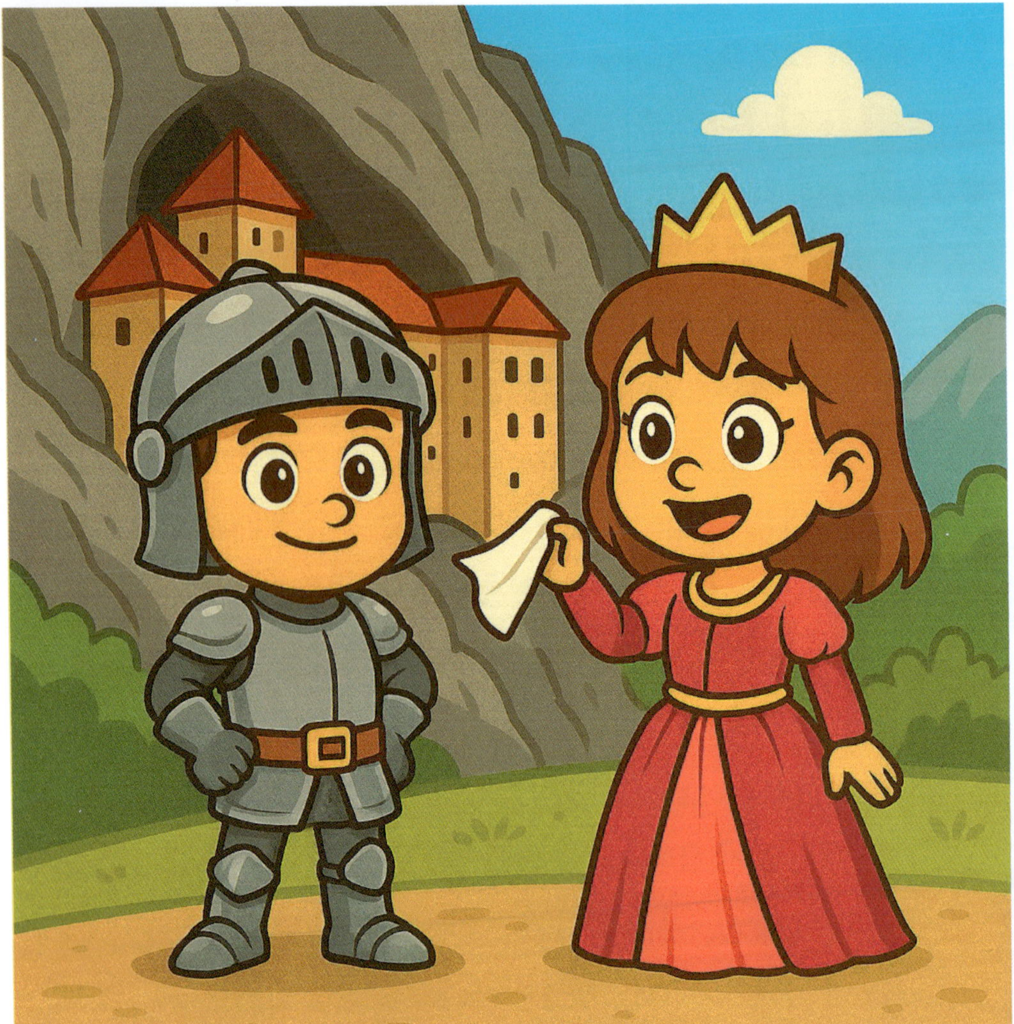

In the Middle Ages, many castles were built across Slovenia. One of the most famous is Predjama Castle, which is tucked right into a giant cave in a cliff. Knights lived here and watched over the lands. One brave knight named Erazem became a legend by hiding from enemies in the castle's secret tunnels. Castles were strong stone homes with towers, moats, and flags flying in the wind. People farmed, made crafts, and told stories about dragons and heroes. These castles remind us of when kings ruled, and knights protected the land.

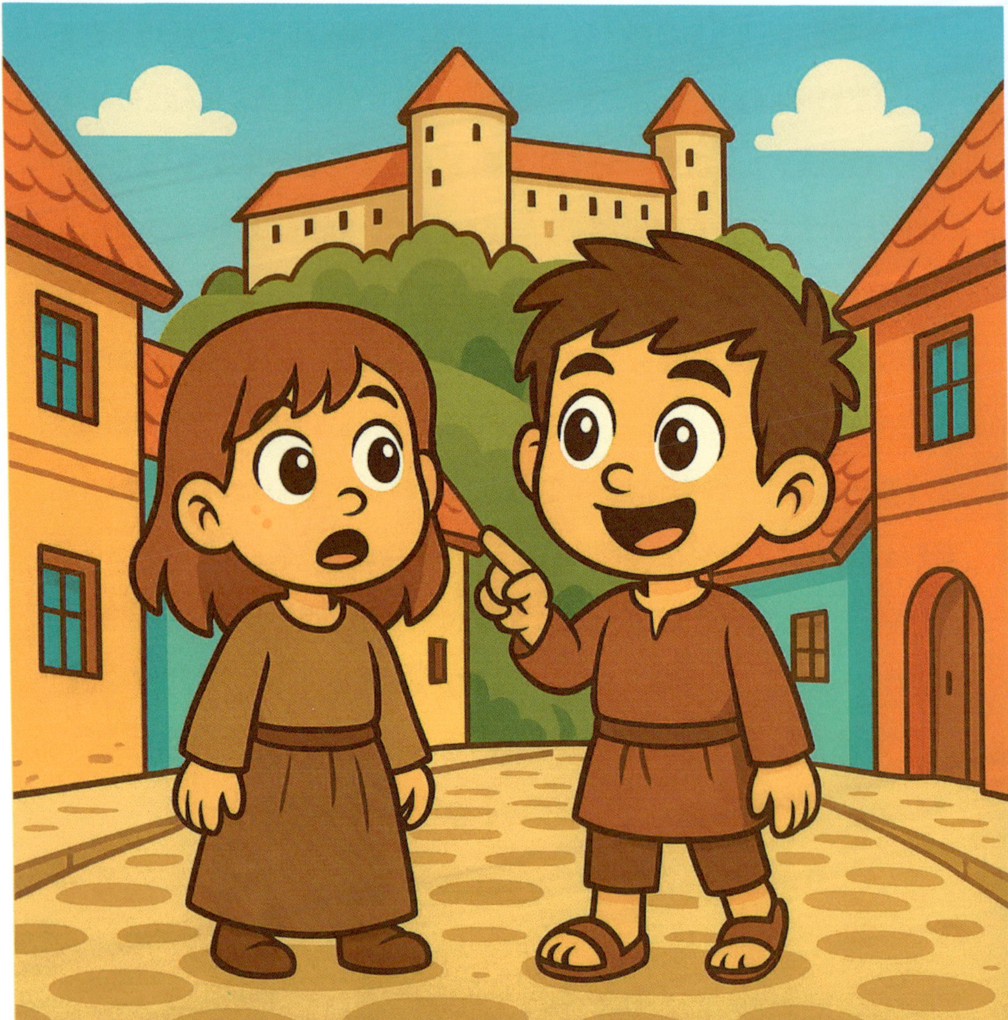

Ptuj is the oldest town in Slovenia, and its history goes back more than 2,000 years. It began as a Roman camp and grew into a medieval town with cobblestone streets and red-roofed houses. The big Ptuj Castle stands on a hill, watching over the Drava River. Long ago, traders came here from all around to sell goods in the market. Today, Ptuj still holds festivals, including one called Kurentovanje. The town's bells, music, and masks bring old traditions to life every year. Walking through Ptuj feels like stepping into the past.

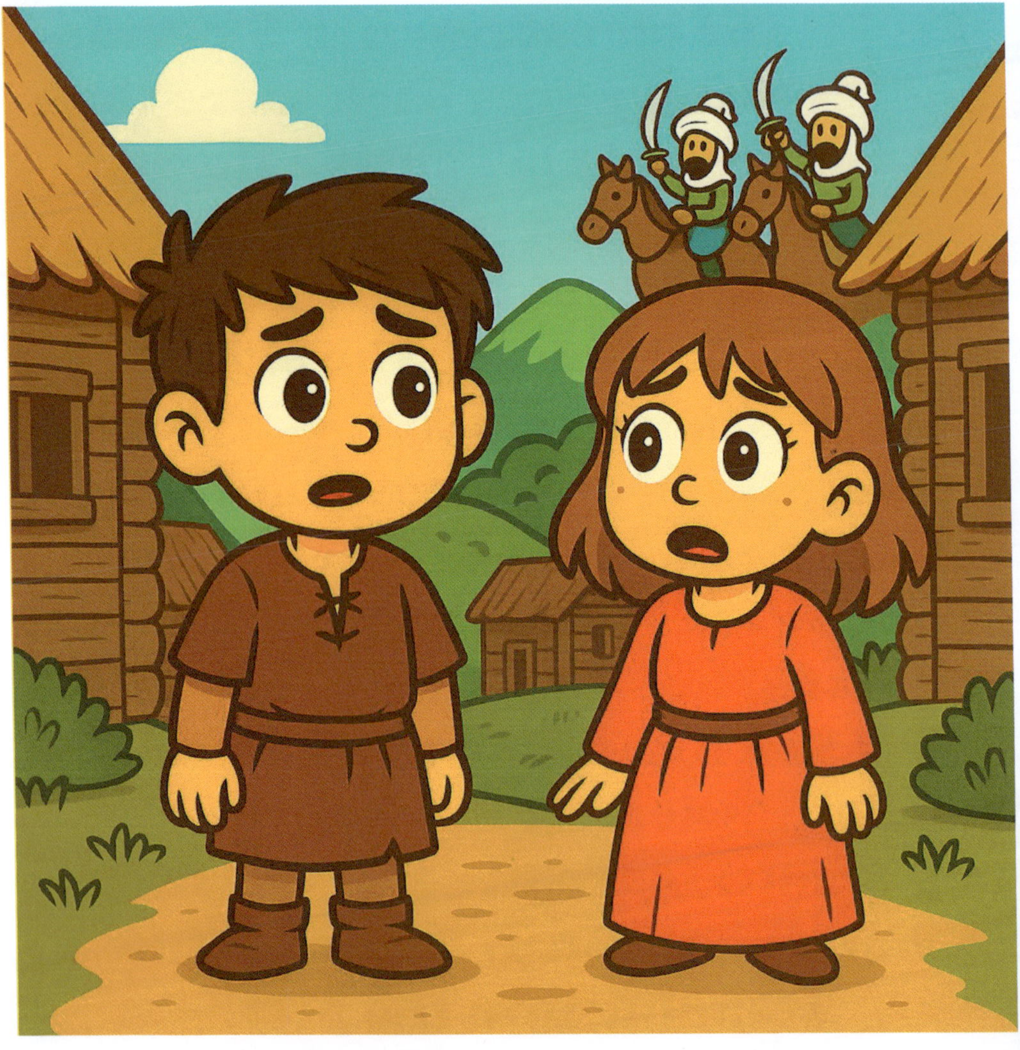

Hundreds of years ago, Slovenia faced attacks from the Ottoman Empire. Villages built watchtowers to warn people when enemies were coming. Families had to run and hide in forests or strong castles. It was a scary time, but Slovenian people stayed strong and brave. They shared stories of heroes who defended the land and helped each other stay safe. These raids changed the way people lived and built their homes. History remembers the courage of the villagers who stood together.

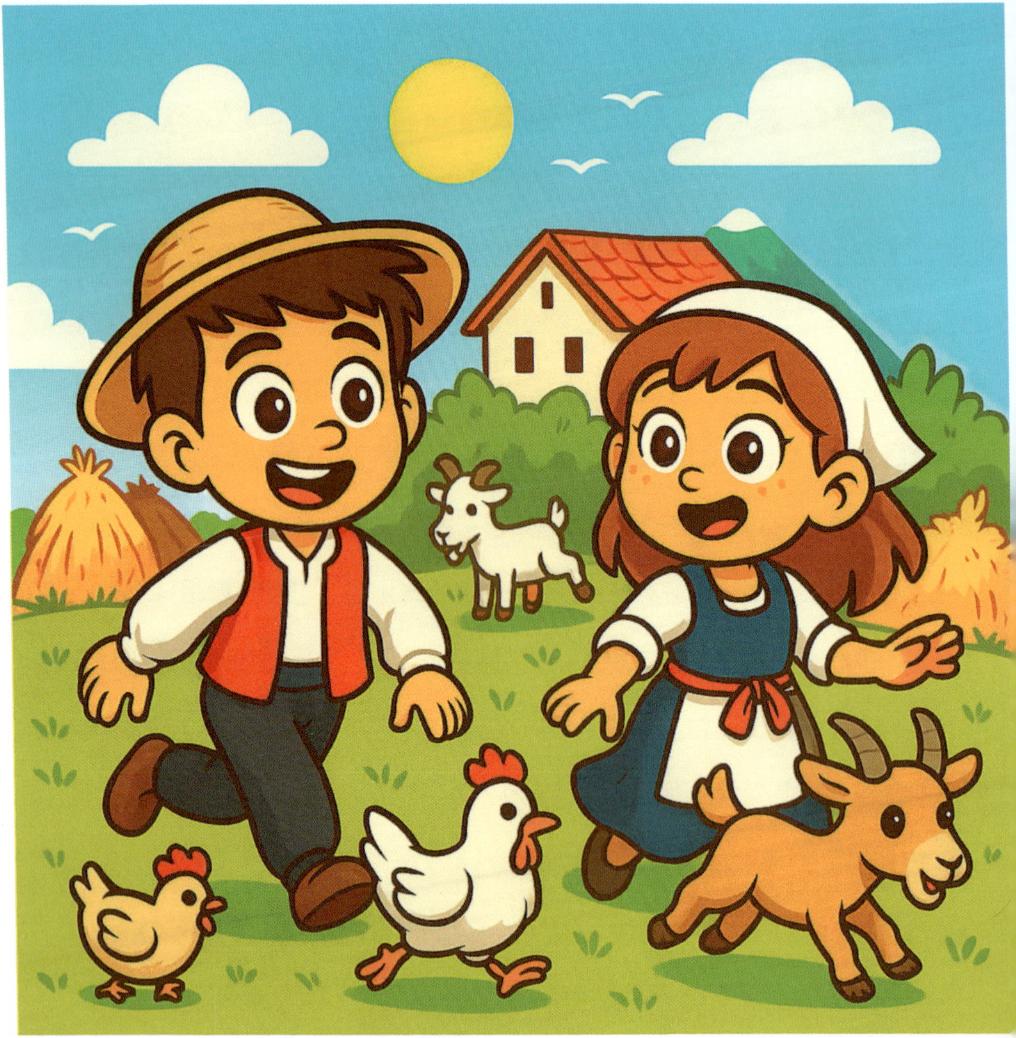

For centuries, Slovenians lived in small villages in the countryside. They grew wheat, raised animals, and made cheese and honey. Families worked and passed down traditions from parents to children. Folk songs, dances, and colorful costumes were part of everyday life. People built cozy homes from wood and stone, with flowers on the windowsills. Even today, you can visit these farms and see how life used to be. The land and the people shaped each other over time.

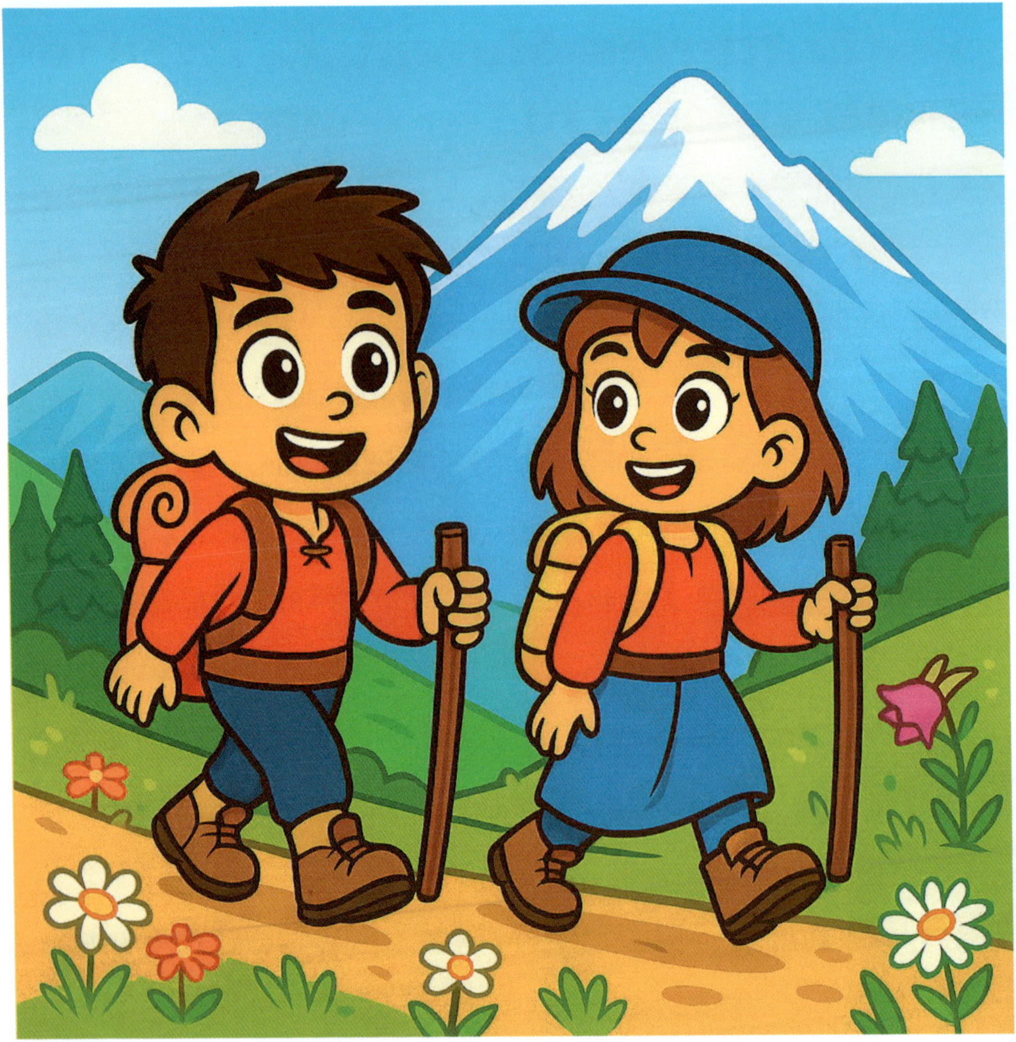

Mount Triglav is the highest mountain in Slovenia and a symbol of the country. It stands tall in the Julian Alps and even appears on the Slovenian flag. Triglav means "three heads," and many Slovenians believe that everyone should climb it once in their life. The mountain is part of Triglav National Park, filled with waterfalls, lakes, and wild animals. Hikers come from all over to enjoy the fresh air and stunning views. In the past, shepherds brought their flocks here in the summer. The mountain has always been a place of pride and peace.

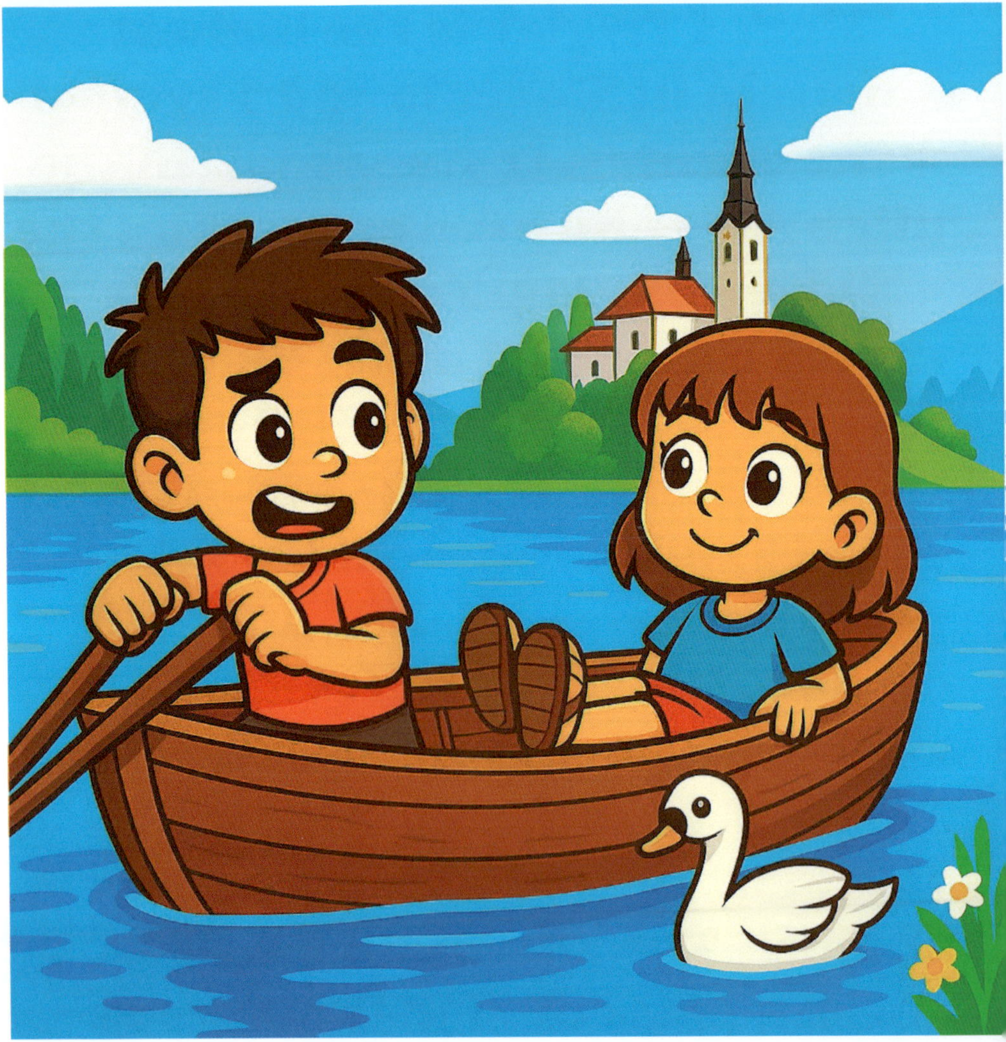

Lake Bled is one of the most magical places in Slovenia. In the middle of the lake is a tiny island with a church, where visitors ring a bell and make a wish. People row special wooden boats called pletna to reach the island. Long ago, this lake was surrounded by legends of fairies and magical creatures. Bled Castle sits high above the water on a cliff and has been watching over the lake for more than 1,000 years. Even today, couples get married on the island and celebrate with cream cake called blejska kremšnita.

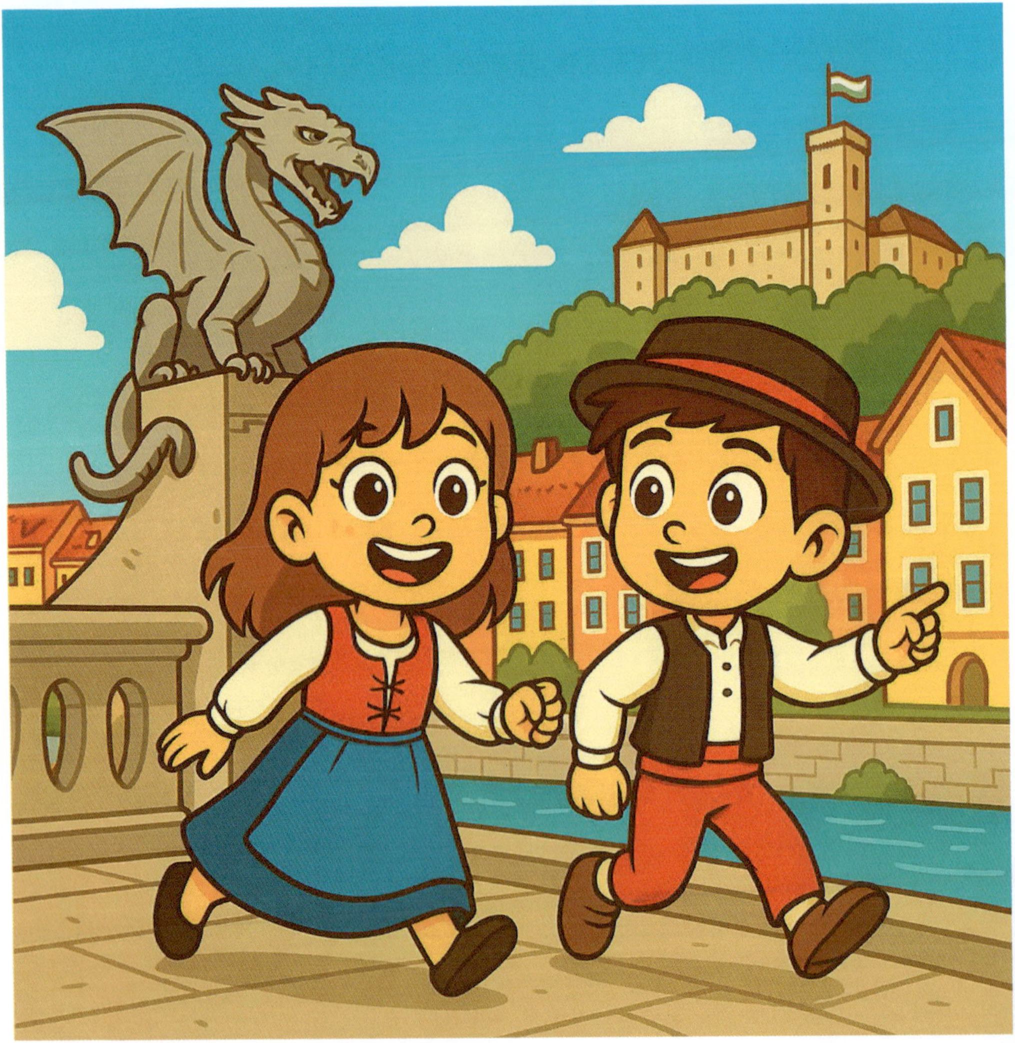

Ljubljana is the capital of Slovenia and one of the greenest cities in Europe. A river winds through the center, with dragons guarding the famous Dragon Bridge. According to legend, the Greek hero Jason fought a dragon here on his journey. The city has charming cafes, playful art, and a castle that watches from above. Many of its buildings were designed by a creative architect named Jože Plečnik. Ljubljana is full of bike paths, music festivals, and friendly people. It's a small city with a big heart, where old myths meet modern magic.

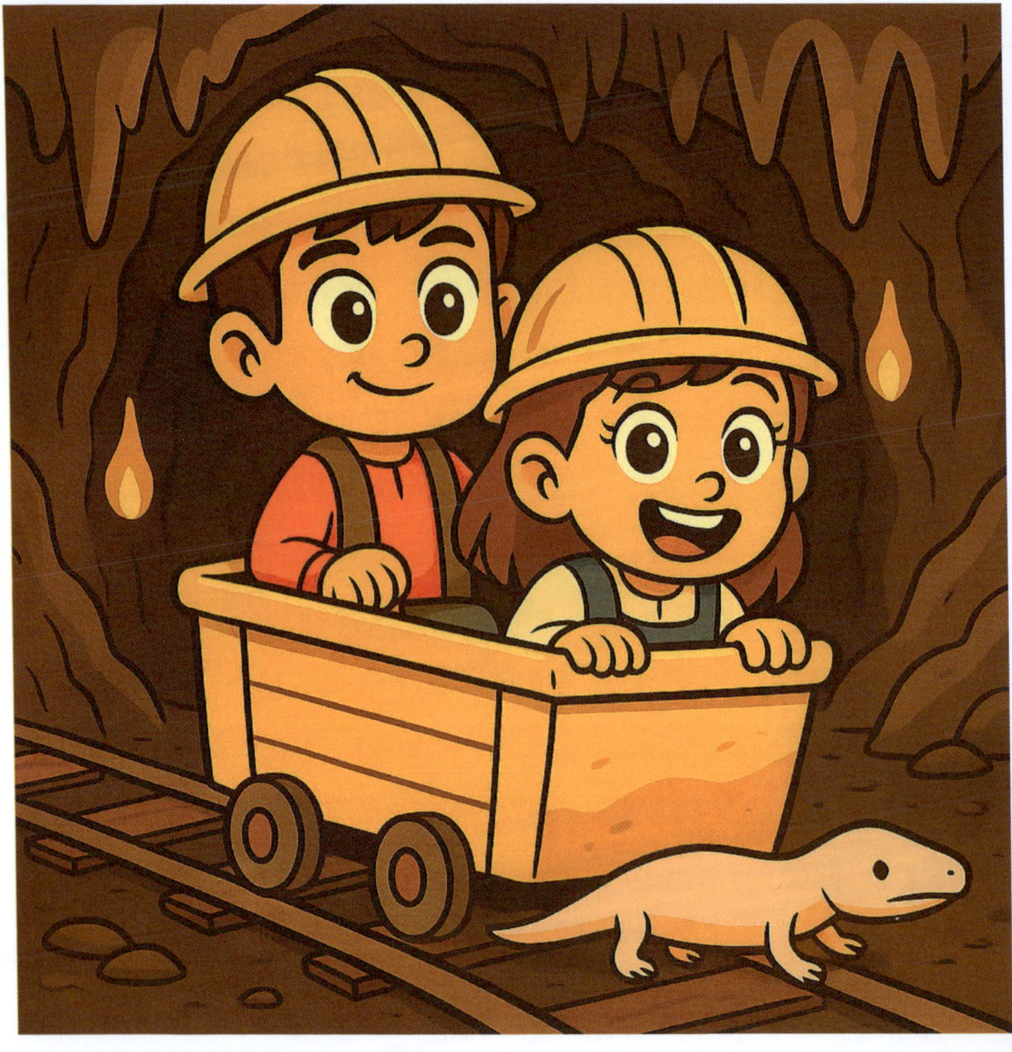

Beneath Slovenia's ground is a hidden world of caves and tunnels. The Postojna Cave is one of the most famous and has over 15 miles of underground passages. Visitors ride a special cave train through tunnels filled with sparkling stone shapes. Inside lives a strange creature called the olm or "baby dragon." It has no eyes and lives in the dark, breathing underwater. These caves formed millions of years ago and are part of the Karst region, which even gave its name to cave landscapes around the world. Exploring them feels like entering another planet.

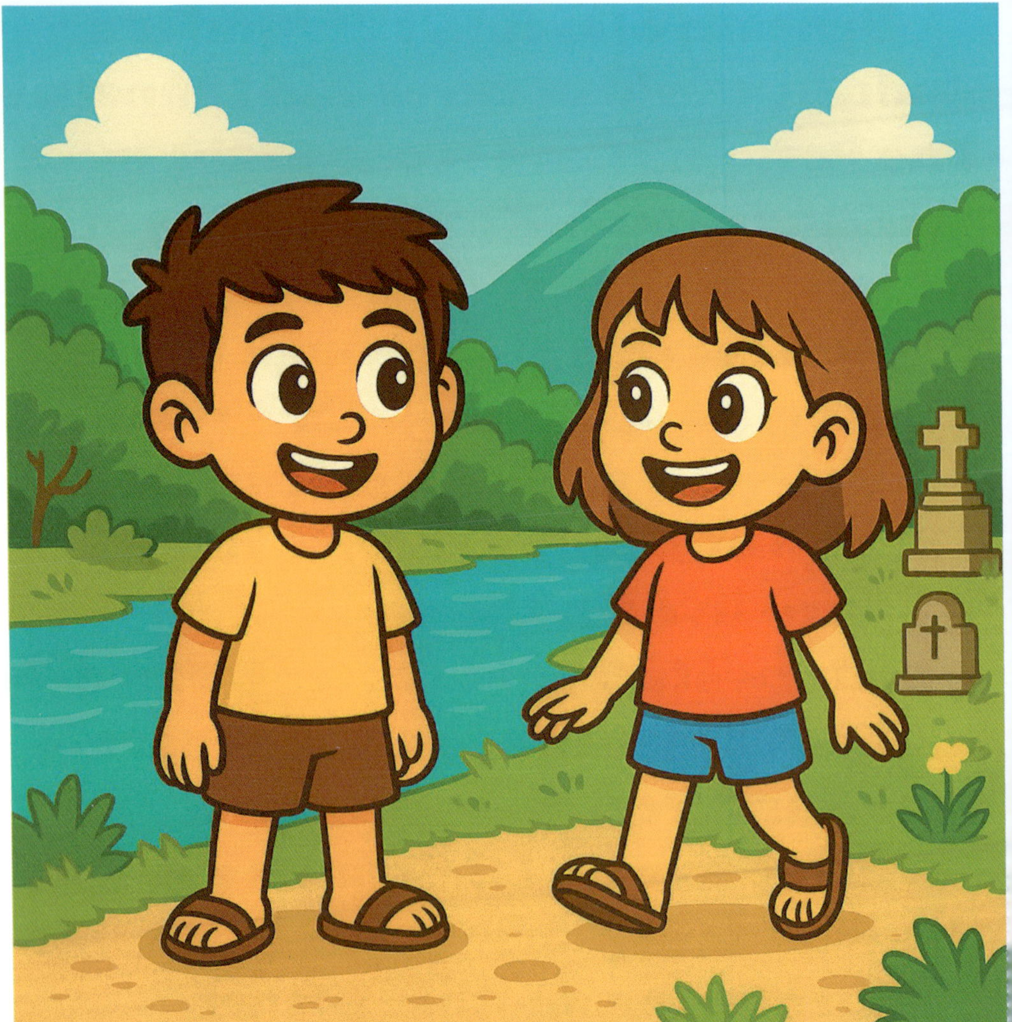

The Soca River is bright blue and flows like a ribbon through western Slovenia. During World War I, fierce battles were fought along its banks. Soldiers from many countries came here during the Isonzo Front, and the mountains echoed with the sounds of war. Today, the area is quiet again, with trails, bridges, and gentle waterfalls. People come to kayak, fish, and hike where history once roared. Memorials and museums help us remember the past and honor those who were here. Nature has healed the land, but the stories remain.

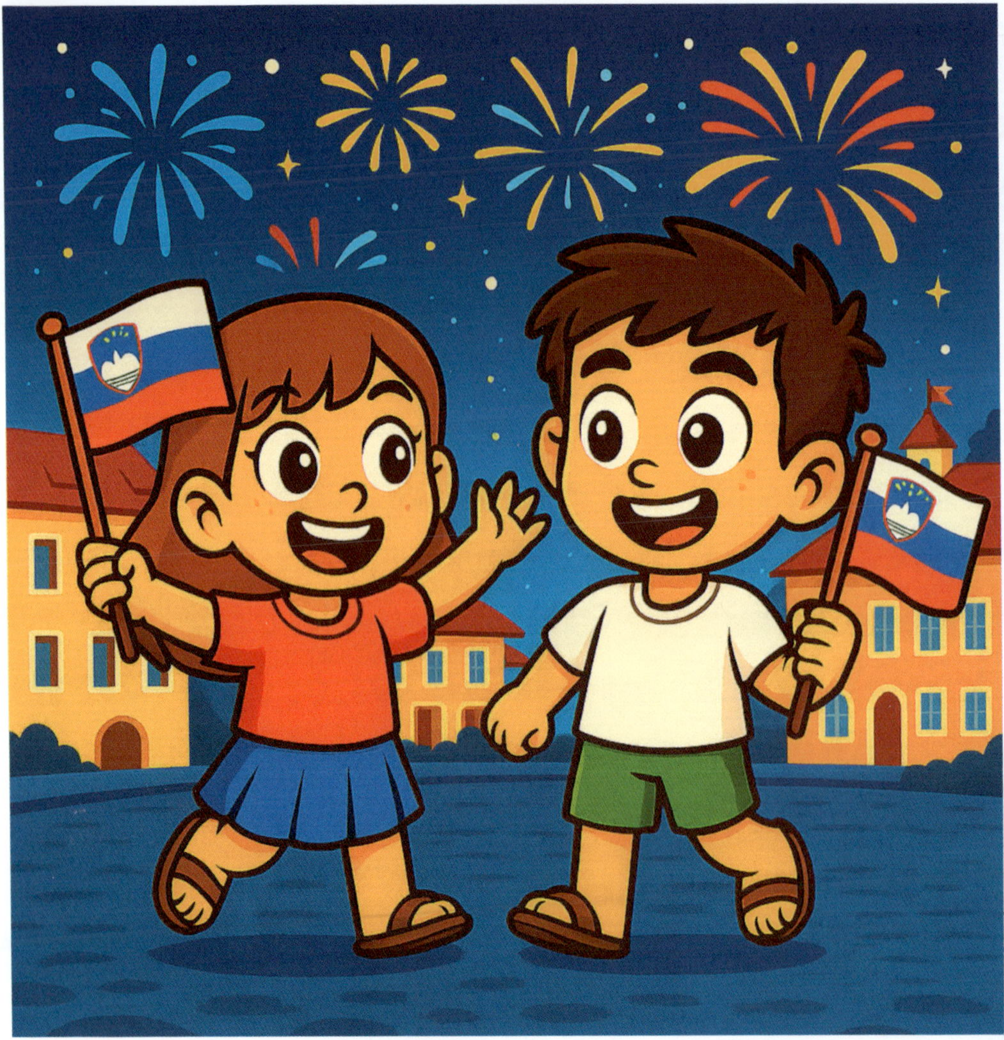

For a long time, Slovenia was part of bigger empires and countries. But in 1991, after many efforts, Slovenia became its own independent nation. People gathered in the streets and cheered as the new flag flew high. The country's first days of freedom were filled with hope and pride. Even though there was a short conflict, Slovenia's independence was quickly recognized by the world. Every year, Slovenians celebrate their freedom on June 25. It's a time to wave flags, sing songs, and feel proud of the country they built together.

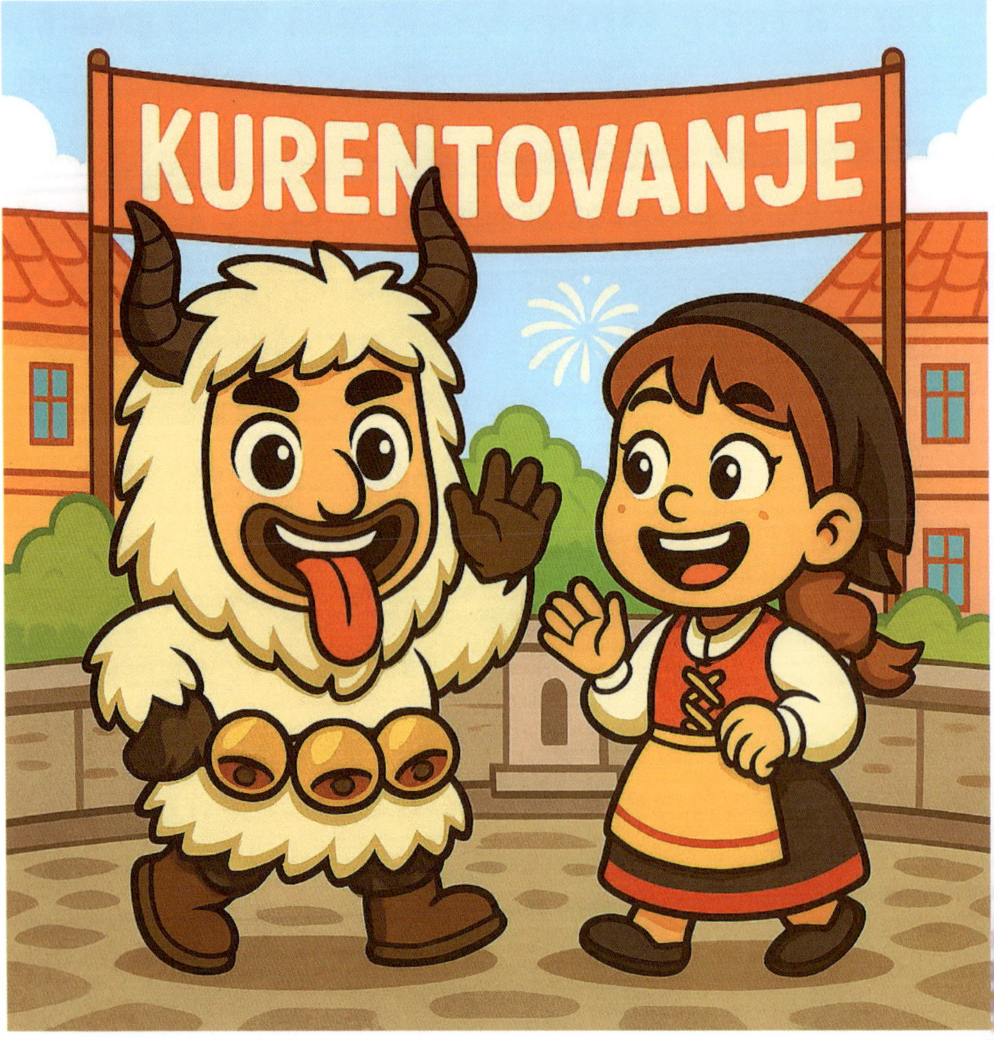
KURENTOVANJE

Every February, the town of Ptuj becomes a parade of joy during Kurentovanje. People wear costumes made of fur, feathers, and loud bells to scare away winter. The Kurent is a traditional figure with a red tongue, big horns, and giant boots. These parades are full of music, laughter, and sweet pastries. Folk dances, storytelling, and old songs are important in Slovenian culture. Kurentovanje is both wild and wonderful, a celebration of old times and new beginnings.

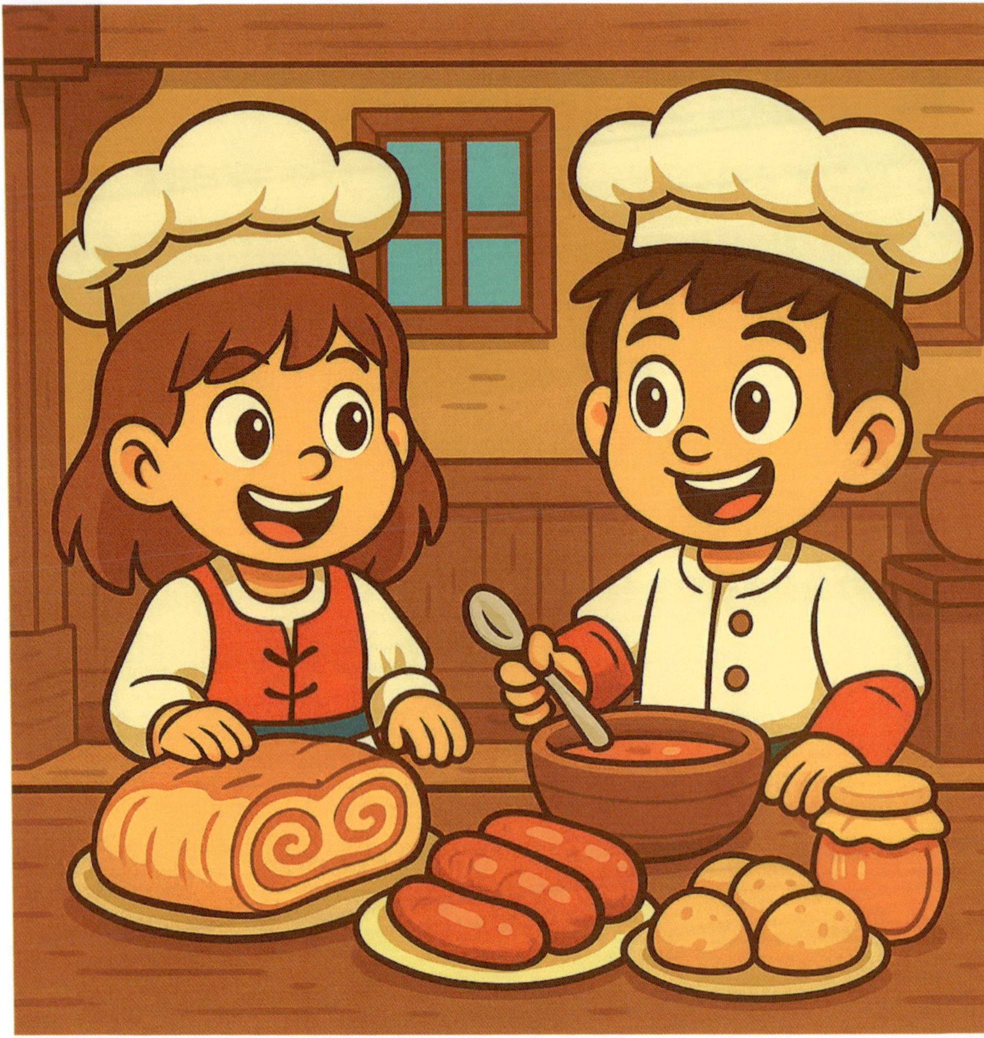

Slovenian food is cozy, hearty, and full of flavor. One famous dessert is potica, a rolled cake filled with walnuts or poppy seeds. People also enjoy sausages, soups, dumplings, and cheeses from mountain farms. Honey has been important in Slovenia for centuries, and beekeeping is a proud tradition. In fact, Slovenia is home to the special Carniolan honeybee. Meals include bread, fresh herbs, and vegetables. Whether in the city or countryside, Slovenians love to gather around the table and share delicious bites with family and friends.

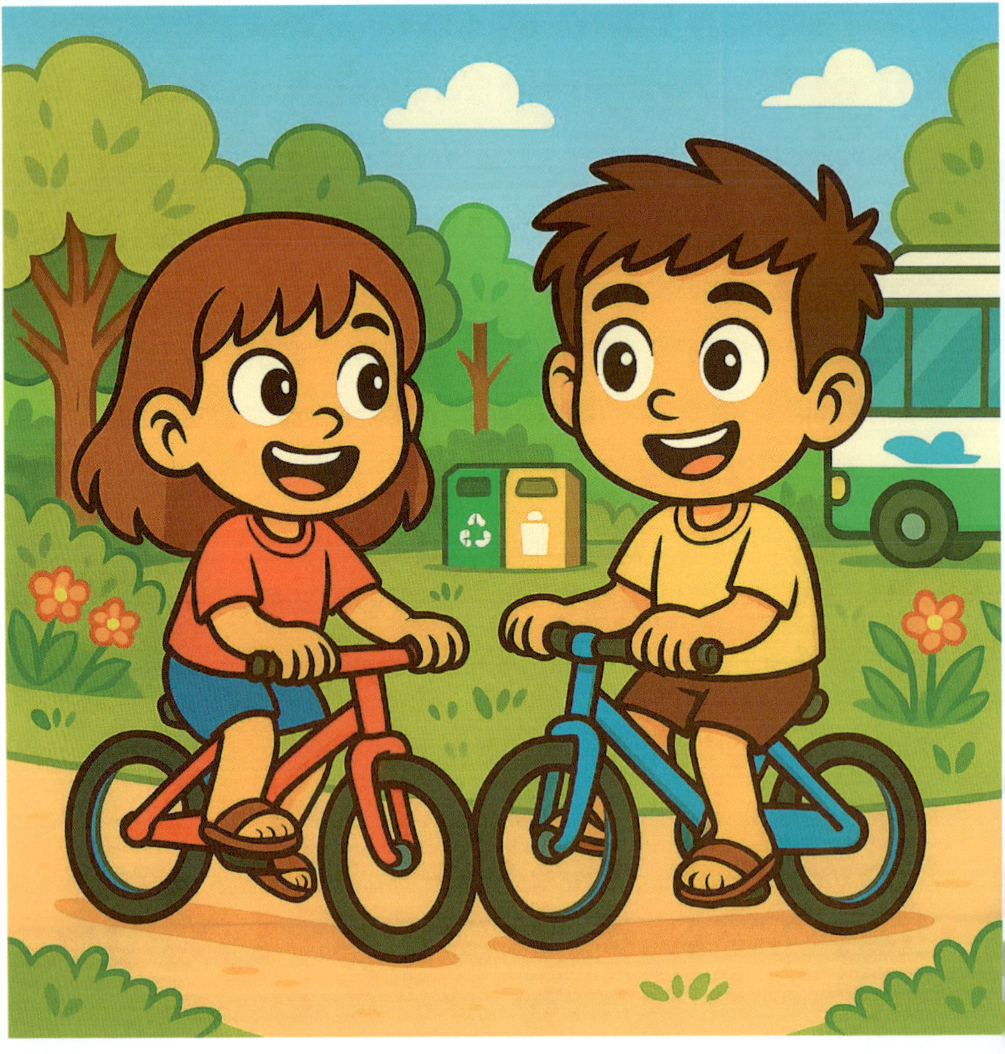

Slovenia is one of the greenest countries in the world. More than half of its land is covered in forests, and many cities work hard to protect the environment. Ljubljana even won the European Green Capital award. People recycle, bike, and use clean energy to take care of nature. National parks and nature reserves protect animals like bears, lynx, and deer. Slovenians believe that living in harmony with nature is part of being a good neighbor. It's a country where birds sing, rivers sparkle, and trees are close by.

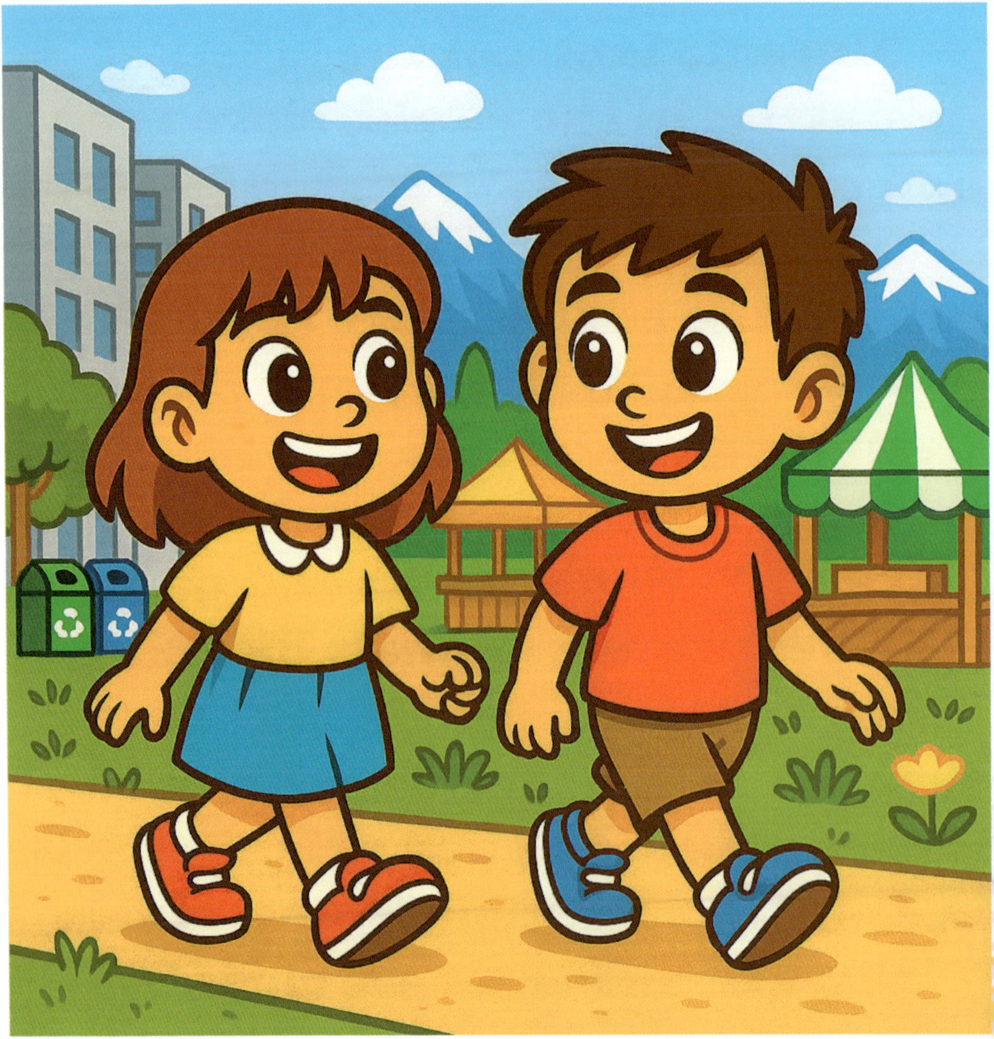

Today, Slovenia is a peaceful and modern country full of color and creativity. Children go to school, play sports, and learn many languages. Families enjoy festivals, concerts, and trips to the mountains or the sea. Cities have museums and playgrounds, while the countryside has farms and hiking trails. People take pride in their culture and look forward to the future. Slovenia is part of the European Union and shares ideas with the world. From its quiet villages to its buzzing cities, this little country keeps growing, learning, and shining.

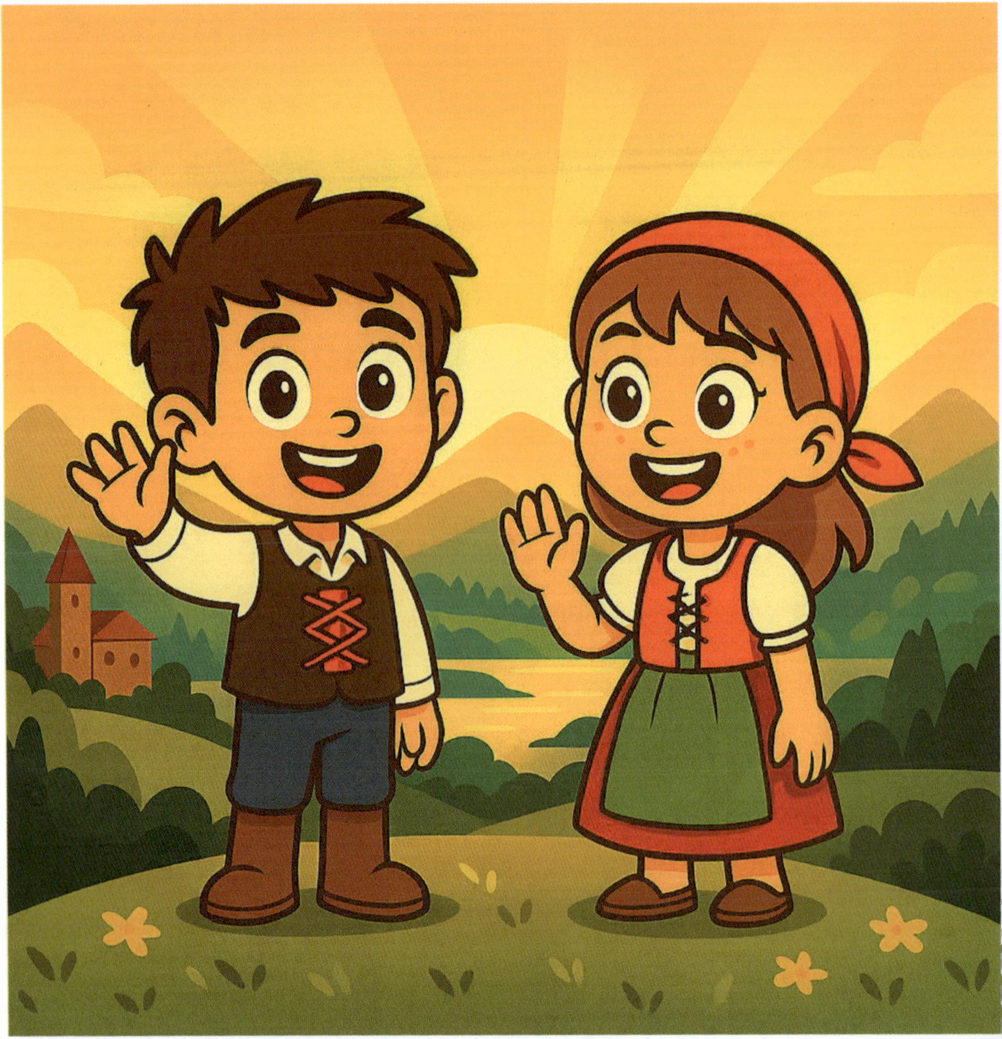

What a journey through Slovenia! We've seen ancient caves, castles, dragon bridges, and cheerful parades. We've learned how brave people made this land their home, how they celebrated, and how they cared for the forests and rivers. Slovenia may be small on the map, but its heart is big and full of wonder. The people say hvala when they want to say thank you. So, hvala for coming along on this adventure. Keep exploring, keep learning, and maybe one day, you'll visit Slovenia in real life. Until then, the stories will stay with you.

Logan Stover is an Author, YouTube Host, & Special Education Teacher from California

**Follow Me
@LearnWithLoganOfficial**
'Learn With Logan' YouTube Channel

I'd Love to Hear From You!

Thank you so much for picking up this book. As an author and educator, I pour my heart into every page, hoping to inspire curiosity and a love for learning. Your support means the world to me, and ***one of the best ways you can help my books reach more readers is by leaving an honest review.***

Whether you loved it, learned something new, or even have suggestions for improvement, I truly appreciate your feedback. Your reviews help other readers discover these stories and support my mission to make history exciting and accessible for everyone—kids, teens, and adults alike.

Monthly Free Book Giveaway!

As a small token of my gratitude, <u>I run monthly giveaways for a free signed copy of one of my books!</u> If you'd like to enter, just send me an email with a screenshot of a photo of the book to *LoganStoverAuthor@Gmail.com*. Every month, I'll randomly select one winner. It's my way of giving back to the amazing readers like you who make this journey possible.

Thank you for being part of this adventure with me. Your support, encouragement, and honest words mean more than you know.

Printed in Dunstable, United Kingdom